TAKING YOUR FINANCIAL PULSE

HOW TO IMPROVE YOUR FINANCIAL HEALTH & BUILD GENERATIONAL WEALTH

ANDREW MASON

Taking your financial pulse: How to improve your financial health & build generational wealth.

Published by Educator Aide®

ISBN-13: 9781736535721

Printed in the United States of America.

DEDICATION

Dedicated to those who are devoted to becoming the hero in their financial health journey.

Table of Contents

A NOTE FROM ANDY......................................18

INTRODUCTION TO THE JOURNEY......................21

CHAPTER 1: **INTRO TO MONEY MANAGEMENT**......25

CHAPTER 2: **BUDGETING BASICS**.......................... 38

CHAPTER 3: **BUILDING A HEALTHY**

BALANCE SHEET..56

CHAPTER 4: **SAVING STRATEGIES**........................ 69

CHAPTER 5: **FORMULATING YOUR VISION**........... 80

CHAPTER 6: **BE YOUR OWN HERO: WALKING YOUR**

WAY TO WEALTH..92

RESOURCES... 100

A Note from Our Legal Team

TERMS AND CONDITIONS

Andrew Mason, AIM Financial, and/or its members, officers, directors, owners, employees, agents, representatives, suppliers, and service providers, provides this book (the "text") for informational purposes only.

NO INVESTMENT ADVICE

The text is for informational purposes only, you should not construe any such information or other material as legal, tax, investment, financial, or other advice. Nothing contained in our text constitutes a solicitation, recommendation, endorsement, or offer by from Andrew Mason, AIM Financial, and/or any third-party service provider to buy or sell any securities or other financial instruments in this or in in any other jurisdiction in which such solicitation or offer would be unlawful under the securities laws of such jurisdiction.

All content in this text is information of a general nature and does not address the circumstances of any individual or entity. Nothing in the text constitutes professional and/or financial advice, nor does any information in the text constitute a comprehensive or complete statement of the matters discussed or the law relating thereto. You alone assume the sole responsibility of evaluating the merits and risks associated with the use of any information or other content in the text before making any decisions based on such information or other content. In exchange for using the text, you agree not to hold Andrew Mason, AIM Financial, or its affiliates or any third-party-adjacent service provider liable for any possible claim for damages arising from any decision you make based on information or other content made available to you through the text.

INVESTMENT RISKS

There are risks associated with investing in securities. Investing in stocks, bonds, exchange traded funds, mutual funds, and money market funds involve risk of loss. Loss of principal is possible. Some high-risk investments may use leverage, which will accentuate gains & losses. Foreign investing involves special risks, including a greater volatility and political, economic and currency risks and differences in accounting methods. A securities or a firm's past investment performance is not a guarantee or predictor of future investment performance.

PREFACE

A Note from Andy

A large percentage of our population doesn't feel empowered by money and there is mainly the energy of fear that haunts so many of our lives. Who can blame us? If it isn’t taxes, it seems like credit card debts and inflation rates are hitting the American family *hard*! *Especially* since 2019. Unfortunately, as a financial advisor, I encounter individuals every day who have (1) been misled or (2) they are not viewing their own financial matters in a way that would give them a better sense of self-worth.

So how do we get better *together*?

For both our children and us, a healthy relationship with finances *is* possible and must be taught intentionally. Allow this journey to be one of restoration between you and your relationship with money. This is my hope for you and those who engage in this powerful learning journey with us.

Whether you have picked up this book at age 18 or 48, my goal is for you to have a healthy vision for your financial health and experience freedom in your relationship with money by establishing the tools, strategies, and approaches that are relevant for living your best life and building your long-term legacy.

As you work your way through the teachings and exercises within this text, remember that there is no "right", "wrong", or "perfect" way to develop your vision for your financial health and long-term wealth.

As I considered the first book I wanted to create, it became clear what any person in the workforce needs right now: **options for how to develop their own unique vision for financial health and generational wealth-building.**

The era of tired formulas and "do it my way" wannabes on the internet talking *at* us is leaving the train station, folks. Next stop: YOU take control and get in the driver's seat with your financial health…once and for all.

When people engage with my book, I want them to feel CONFIDENCE. I want to see you unafraid to take the tools and strategies I am sharing with you and GO FOR IT! Try new things. Learn, un-learn, and re-learn. It's okay to prioritize yourself so that you come first. I want your vision to be so clear by the end of this text that you confidently pay yourself first – and never look back.

My objective… This is my first book. I am a visionary and dreamer, but I have kept my vision for this resource quite simple:

To help people from age 18-48 ***implement a clear vision for their financial health.***

For each reader to experience freedom with money by adapting the tools, strategies, and approaches that are most relevant for ***your abundant life and long-term legacy.***

Here's to your financial health journey. May it be fruitful through every season.

Sincerely,

Andy

INTRODUCTION: THE JOURNEY…

Welcome to my interactive text on taking your financial pulse so you can prioritize your financial health while building generational wealth. In this text, we will explore, learn, and apply a multitude of core concepts together.

As you work through some of the template suggestions I have created for you throughout this book, remember that your process for reflecting on your weekly or monthly balance sheet should suit YOU! My hope is that my tools give you some foundational guidance to help you get started with a financial health vision and ongoing wealth building systems that will work for you and your desired lifestyle.

In addition, this interactive learning text is meant to be marked up and carried with you if you choose! The chapters don't even have to be utilized in any specific order. Of course, we have organized them to help build and scaffold your learning, but there are certainly concepts, exercises, and templates that may resonate with you more than others. Try your best not to get overwhelmed and begin with one step at a time.

Here is a look at the order of our topics:

i. **INTRO TO MONEY MANAGEMENT** A compelling connection exists between our childhoods and financial health and vision for our legacies. In this chapter, learn what makes your own personal finances tick…and what ticks you off about money.

ii. **BUDGETING BASICS** Budgeting can significantly help you establish boundaries, however, a budget is a constant moving target that is purely a snapshot in time so most aren't willing to put together a budget. Learn how budgeting can support growth, but also cause stagnation financially if not approached with clarity.

iii. **BUILDING A HEALTHY BALANCE SHEET** In this chapter, we will explore what it means to be "balance sheet wealthy" and why it is so important in our financial health journeys.

iv. **SAVING STRATEGIES** The purpose of saving is to have different buckets of money. The sooner you start with your savings strategies, the more compounding effects you'll experience.

v. **FORMULATING YOUR VISION** As you grow and learn, the strategies you implement *should* change and adapt; what will carry your legacy is your vision and a continual engagement with your financial journey.

vi. **WALKING YOUR WAY TO WEALTH** Everyone has a different vision of what they want their financial wealth and health to be. We want you to enjoy life! Let's envision *how* to make it happen for your most desirable life and legacy.

INTRO TO MONEY MANAGEMENT

CHAPTER 1

What is financial health? In this text you will hear me define and share key terms in every chapter, and to begin this journey I would like to introduce a concept I have been working to develop across multiple decades through serving my clients as their advisor: **financial health**.

Sometimes, we have neglected important verbiage that is necessary for our lexicon when it comes to talking about money. We tend to be binary in our thinking – delineating budgetary items as "good" or "bad" and assets and liabilities as "negative" or "positive" choices.

I want to challenge this status quo. Why?

Financial planning is a *journey*. Like our fitness journeys when we speak of our physical health, it can prove dangerous and, even harmful, to speak about our finances so definitively.

Because the markets are often driven by extenuating factors that are not within our own locust of control, this provides another reason to look at the *health* of our finances. This models an important differentiating language factor. Let's unpack some examples:

1. *In the area of long-term investments, I am looking for ways to improve my **financial health**.*

2. *My **financial health** is suffering a bit right now with cashflow due to some credit card debt.*

3. *Our **financial health** as it relates to saving is promising, given our strategy of utilizing certificates of deposit (CD's).*

Without the terminology *financial health*, here are some common examples you may have even heard your own brain or mouth articulating over the years:

1. *I have nothing contributed to my investments.*

2. *I'm broke.*

3. *I'm rich! I just dumped a bunch of cash into a high-yield CD!*

The main difference you will see by adopting the terminology of ***financial health*** is not subconsciously talking yourself out of what is your birthright.

What do I mean by this?

You may have heard the terms ***scarcity mindset*** and ***abundance mindset*** over the years. The heart of a scarcity mindset is that someone else must lose for you to win. It can also manifest as an internal narrative that *you* have to lose or sacrifice before you can win. Whereas, an abundance mindset is centered around beliefs that you are worthy of being paid well, living a wealthy life, and that there is always more than enough provided for you.

Our mind and our words are powerful. And if we are not careful, we just might talk ourselves out of what we are worthy of having in our bank accounts.

Using the terminology ***financial health*** will help provide a new way to structure your mindset and your actions around financial planning and money, in general. In addition, my proposed terminology comes from a place that allows you to get very specific of the different paths by which you can create wealth for your life.

We often limit our financial opportunities by making a non-specific, broad generalization about our overall finances, as opposed to being more specific like the ***financial health*** examples we began with in the chapter.

STOP & JOT

Take a moment to reflect on the following questions. As you work through this text, please know that each set of *Stop & Jot* questions are designed to help you build out your vision for your optimal financial health.

1. How often do you spend time focusing on what is *working* in your finances? Why or why not?

2. Identify 1 strategy you currently use consistently for saving. How is it working for you and why does it work for your budgeting style?

3. It is 10 years in the future, and you are living your dream life! What are the things you do every day? Who is with you? How do you earn money?

→ **DREAM BIG!**

THE MONEY MANAGEMENT CONVERSATION...

I always remind my clients (especially those who are business owners!) of the following:

→ When you pay yourself first, it gives you a sense of purpose.

I know, I know...This is easier said than done! There is a common phrase floating in the atmosphere that may help keep you centered on your financial health journey: *We are human beings, not human DO-ings.* Money simply provides us the access to live life in the ways we choose.

All too often, I encounter individuals who forget to enjoy the spoils of their hard work. When we are present with each breath we take and every move we make, it helps put money wins or worries into perspective.

Well, now I've let the cat out of the bag. Let's talk **money wins** and **money worries**.

It's helpful to understand our current mindsets with money as a path to understanding why we manage our assets the way we do.

STOP & JOT

Take a moment to reflect on the following questions. As you work through this text, please know that each set of *Stop & Jot* questions are designed to help you build out your vision for your optimal financial health.

1. Which do you tend to fixate on *first* when it comes to your bank accounts: how *much* you have or how *little* you have? *Take time to reflect on what this makes you aware of regarding your current mindset.* Does something need to shift?

Next, we will examine your current mindset around what is a "win" and what is a "worry" when it comes to your financial health. Here is an example before you try the reflection exercise.

MONEY WINS/WORRIES **EXAMPLE A*

WIN	WORRY
$500 per week in savings	18k overall credit card debt
$250 per month to 401k account; employer matching	$450 per month car loan payment
3k tax refund	$200 per month student loan
New credit card limit increased with travel rewards points program	Cost of living increases due to increase in property taxes

Figure 1.1.

Before you spend time reflecting on your *own* money wins and money worries, let's unpack Example A so you can get an idea of the psychology behind the exercise:

→ Our t-chart fixates on the wins! I highly recommend checking any negative fixations on lack at the door. Yes, we must be realistic when examining our net worth and debt worth; our liquid assets and those that are inaccessible (or non-existent). This said, I believe in taking every measure you can to further enhance your money mindset.

The thoughts we share with the world via our mind are powerful. Choose your thoughts wisely! Notice when you are fixating on the lack vs. the abundance in your life.

With Example A, I can begin to formulate the following:

→ They have a **short-term** and **long-term savings strategy** in place.

→ They like to **take advantage of win-wins** where their own contributions can be matched and/or rewarded.

→ They may need to employ some **strategies for paying down low-interest** and **high-interest debts**.

Next, I want you to consider how honest you are being as you try the exercise for yourself. What comes up for you as you write your wins and worries? Do you experience shame around anything you wrote down? **Noticing** your reactions and responses to the different questions and exercises throughout this text is just as important as completing the learning activities themselves.

If I were in the shoes of Example A, I would start to consider how my *Money Wins/Worries* chart aligns with my overall vision for my life.

There's something else I would consider for Example A. I'm getting curious about their life. We certainly don't have all the information about Example A's income, assets, debts, etc. However, based solely on the contributions to savings and their 401k, they seem to be a person who has a bit of insight about long-term saving.

I get curious about their debts and wonder if they are really getting to enjoy their day-to-day life due to money being tied up in contributions and debt payments every month? I would ask Example A: ***Are you paying yourself first?***

Let's begin to assess your current wins and worries to build your custom blueprint for improving your financial health.

Your turn to try on the next page!

MONEY WINS/WORRIES

WIN	WORRY

Figure 1.2.

BUILDING YOUR BLUEPRINT

In this text we are working towards establishing your vision for optimal financial health.

In our *Intro to Money Management* (Chapter 1), we have learned the following terms:

→ **financial health**

→ **scarcity mindset**

→ **abundance mindset**

→ **money wins**

→ **money worries**

We also spent some time working with reflection questions (*Stop & Jots*) and exercises designed to bring more awareness of your current narratives to the forefront as develop your blueprint.

In the next chapter, I will introduce you to my ***C.A.S.H. Financial Health Framework*** that can be applied to any type of budget.

BUDGETING BASICS

CHAPTER 2

What is the C.A.S.H. philosophy? Following the COVID-19 crisis, I decided to develop my financial health framework: C.A.S.H. Why? I realized how many people were reeling from the impact of the pandemic and other global crises.

Sometimes tragedy can cause us to think rationally when it comes to our budget. Perhaps we have all experienced irrational thinking with our finances on some level, too. Here is the heart of my message in this book if you receive nothing else:

It's all about being the **hero** in your own story. Getting in the driver's seat with your finances and taking back control. Let's talk through our graphic and hop into our learning together in this section.

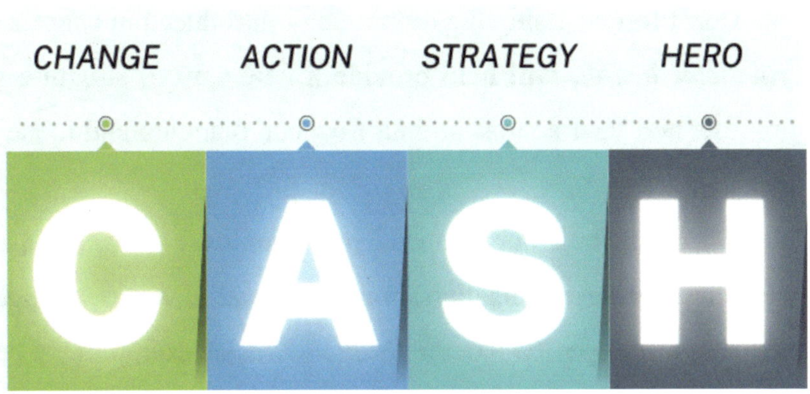

Figure 1.3.

At the **hero** phase of our financial health framework, you are monitoring, adjusting, and realigning as necessary to your financial health vision. Heroes are visionaries, and as the hero of your own financial story, you deserve to nourish and grow your vision.

The process can be applied to any situation by engaging the following protocol:

- Identify the element you are seeking to **change**.
    - *Why is it important to you?*
    - *How does it align with your financial health vision?*
- What **action** can you take in the short-term to impact the change you seek?
    - *Is this action high leverage?*
    - *Is the action manageable?*
- How might you consider a long-term **strategy** that will solidify your goal for change being accomplished?

Don't forget: Using the terminology introduced in chapter one, ***financial health,*** will help provide a new way to structure your mindset and your actions around financial planning and money, in general.

We often limit our financial opportunities by making a non-specific, broad generalization about our overall finances, as opposed to being more specific like the ***financial health*** examples we began with in this book.

THE C.A.S.H. FINANCIAL HEALTH FRAMEWORK:

A STEP-BY-STEP GUIDE

Step 1: CHANGE

CHANGE is about reflecting on your current financial mindset and identifying areas where you feel the need for *change*. This could include attitudes towards spending, saving, investing, or any other aspect of personal finance.

I also encourage you to consider the impact of your current financial mindset on your long-term goals and aspirations. Acknowledge the need for change and commit to embracing a more positive and proactive approach to managing your finances.

Step 2: ACTION

Taking ACTION is all about developing a plan of action to address the areas of your financial mindset that require improvement. This could involve setting specific, achievable goals related to saving, investing, debt reduction, or any other financial priority.

You may consider implementing practical steps to support your plan, such as creating a budget, seeking financial education, or consulting with a professional advisor. Take ownership of your financial journey and commit to consistent action towards positive change.

Step 3: STRATEGY

When you enact the STRATEGY step of the *CASH Financial Health Framework*, you may want to identify specific strategies and tools that align with your financial goals and the areas you wish to improve. This could involve exploring different investment options, debt repayment strategies, or ways to increase your income.

As you will hear me share my honest opinions on budgeting later in this chapter, I want you to tailor any of your strategies to suit your individual circumstances and preferences, ensuring that the strategies you choose are realistic and sustainable for the long term. Most of all: that they are relevant in making you the hero in your own story!

Step 4: HERO

Look at you embracing the concept of becoming the HERO in your own vision for financial health and generational wealth!

Please…Recognize that you have the power to shape your financial future through intentional decision-making and a clear focus on your vision for financial health.

Your vision will support you in cultivating a mindset of empowerment and resilience, viewing challenges as opportunities for growth and learning. Commit to being an active participant in your financial journey and strive to inspire positive change within yourself and others.

By using the guidance of the *CASH Financial Health Framework*, you can gain a deeper understanding of your financial mindset and develop a clear roadmap for achieving greater stability, security, and prosperity.

This framework empowers you to take control of your financial well-being and work towards building a legacy of generational wealth through intentional action and strategic planning.

STOP & JOT

Take a moment to reflect on the following questions. As you work through this text, remember that each set of *Stop & Jot* questions are designed to help you build out your vision for your optimal financial health.

1. Let's go deeper with the ***C.A.S.H. Financial Health Framework.*** What are 2 habits you will be implementing to support the **change** you are seeking?

2. I am all about **you** paying ***you*** FIRST. How are you becoming the **hero** in your own story each day? What shifts are you noticing in your life?

3. It is 10 years in the future, and you are living your dream life! (*Yes! There is a reason you are seeing this question again!)* What are the things you do every day? Who is with you? How do you earn money? → **HINT: Get specific about your long-term strategy that has developed generational wealth.**

BUDGETING IS YOUR PERSONAL PREFERENCE [*IMO…*]

Remember what I tell my clients:

→ When you pay yourself first,
it gives you a sense of purpose.

In my opinion…[*IMO*]. I love how Gen Y and Gen Z have normalized shortened acronyms as a core part of how we all communicate. What influence!

Speaking of Generation Z, one anecdote I want to share as we jump headfirst into budgeting happened at a local café where I overheard the two baristas (both under age 25, approximately) discussing how they *never* go to the store for groceries.

"Yea girl. I just Instacart that!"

If only managing the ins and outs, ebbs, and flows, with mountains and valleys of our budgets were as easy as the swipe of a button!

Well…it can be. With the age of technology advancing as never before, we have never been more equipped to manifest the wealth one can learn about in the Napoleon Hill timeless text Think and Grow Rich:

"Keep in mind the fact that there are only two known elements in the whole universe, energy, and matter. It is well known fact that matter may be broken down into units of molecules, atoms, and electrons. There are units of matter which may be isolated, separated, and analyzed." (p. 252)

Taking the example of energy and matter will help us explore the concept of **budgeting**. Let's think of the concept as "**the energy and matter of budgeting**".

If only managing the ins and outs, ebbs, and flows, with mountains and valleys of our budgets were as easy as the swipe of a button!

Budgeting tools such as auto tagging your expenses in a bank account or acquiring a life insurance policy as an investment/savings are strategies we utilize as consumers. These strategies essentially make up our approach to budgeting. The "matter" – which can be broken into multiple parts.

So where does the **energy** concept come into play? Consider where you place your time and thought space.

→ Are you constantly worried about when you get paid or the debt collectors?

→ Do you look at stock or trade platforms daily?

→ How often are you finding yourself worried and/or celebrating or bragging when it comes to your financial health vision?

These are examples of questions many people ask themselves. Or even have on repeat in their head. [*If that is you…it will be okay!*]

Where our attention goes, our energy flows. This helps illustrate that we can take advantage of all the technology and money management tools, platforms, etc. However, if our energy is still fixated upon actions filled with worry, greed, anxiety, and fears, we will inevitably attract more of those same energies into our experience.

BUDGETING BASICS:

STRAIGHTFORWARD PROS & CONS

I may already sound like a broken record…but I must remind you again: nothing will feel quite as effective as a strategy for wealth-building (and self-worth!) as **paying yourself *first.*** There is a behavioral aspect and relationship we all have with money. Our behaviors influence our spending habits.

How we view the world, the concept of value, and what we find as worthy of our earnings are all factors that drive how we interact with money.

How we interact with money and how we *think* about it are attributes of any budget's foundation. What we connect money to within our lives.

An example…If I start getting a flat tire every 30 miles, I'm going to decide I *must* do something differently because there is absolutely no way I'm stopping every 30 miles!

Behaviorally, I would get very curious about *what* is happening with my car:

Is it the car?

The tires?

The route?

The driver?

For some reason, I observe that it is harder for us humans to embrace this same curiosity with our finances. We play games. We avoid logging into accounts. Dodge phone calls from the bank. Get over-anxious about repaying debt or paying taxes.

We must begin viewing our own journey to wealth as an adaptive experience. Pivoting is your *power*! Let's learn to get on the balcony *and* the dance floor with our financial health.

This is how I might describe the dance I advise you to have with the concept of **budgeting**. Never get so locked in with the dance floor that you can't transition to the balcony and vice versa. Most of all, I believe *you* hold the keys to your financial health vision and *you* are the hero of your own story. As such, I must trust you and you must trust yourself to move forward in the best ways you see possible for your path.

This said, I'll share my "top 2" with you:

MY TOP 2 "PROS" OF BUDGETING

- Helps you establish your boundaries for saving and spending habits.
- Develops consistent and predictable rhythms and routines for building wealth.

MY TOP 2 "CONS" OF BUDGETING

- Can be a constant moving target that is purely a snapshot in time, so most aren't willing to put together a complex budget. Be honest about your capacity!
- Budgeting can cause stagnation. We can lose our edge with hunting out the latest investment strategies or trends, get locked in to learning from only the same handful of voices in thought leadership, and worst of all, we may be missing opportunities to build more generational wealth for us and our loved ones.

THE CASH MONEY CASE STUDY

To bring more awareness into your money mindset as you build your blueprint to commit to your financial health vision, I would like to share this case study with you for your analysis and reflection.

SARAH'S CASH MONEY CONUNDRUM

Sarah is a 28-year-old marketing professional who is finding herself in a tight spot when her car unexpectedly broke down. The costly repairs have piled up and she is faced with the urgent need for cash. Due to her current situation, she has been hesitant about her ability to stick to a budget. Even despite having a stable income, Sarah has always struggled with some impulsive spending habits and has never really maintained a consistent budget. I suppose she's like many of us: our money is not a problem until it is a problem.

The idea of restricting her spending and expenses to have enough cash for the car repairs seems overwhelming and she's unsure if she can resist the temptation of unnecessary purchases. Feeling incredibly overwhelmed, Sarah decides to seek advice from a financial counselor to develop a realistic budgeting plan that will allow her to cover the unexpected expenses of her car repairs without compromising her other expenses that she is responsible for.

After consulting with the financial counselor, Sarah now has a better understanding of the importance of budgeting and understanding your balance sheet. With the practical guidance of developing a balance sheet process every month, aligned with her income and spending, she is creating a personalized approach that aligns with her current income needs.

By implementing the recommended strategies, such as tracking her expenses, prioritizing essential costs, and setting aside a portion of her income for savings and investments, Sarah feels more confident in managing her finances. With the support of the budgeting plan and ongoing guidance from the financial counselor, Sarah is successfully navigating the unexpected car situation! Not only is she "taking care of business" – she is developing a healthier outlook with her relationship with money.

STOP & JOT

Take a moment to reflect on the following questions. As you work through this text, please remember that each set of *Stop & Jot* questions are designed to help you build out your vision for your optimal financial health.

1. Let's go deeper with what Sarah is experiencing. Think of a time when you were in a financial crunch or crisis. What tends to be your go-to response?

2. How might you coach yourself through a financial situation that causes you anxiety?

In this case study, Sarah's experience highlights the common challenge of needing cash urgently while lacking confidence in maintaining a budget. Through proactive steps and professional guidance, she was able to overcome her concerns and achieve financial stability, underscoring the value of personalized budgeting strategies.

In building your blueprint, remember that the best budgeting strategy (*in my opinion!*) is your own personalized and empowered approach to budgeting where you are the hero of your story.

BUILDING YOUR BLUEPRINT

In this text we are working towards establishing your vision for optimal financial health. In our *Budgeting Basics* (Chapter 2), we have explored the following terms:

→ **financial health**

→ **CASH Financial Health Framework**

→ **budgeting**

→ **the energy and matter of budgeting**

We also spent some time working with reflection questions (*Stop & Jots*) and exercises (like Sarah's "*Cash Money Case Study"*!) designed to bring more awareness of your current narratives to the forefront as develop your blueprint.

In the next chapter, we will discuss what it means to build a healthy balance sheet.

BUILDING A HEALTHY BALANCE SHEET

CHAPTER 3

Healthy. Such a common word we likely use in our vocabulary multiple times a week in different contexts. It reminds me of the stories from numerous texts about *how* you build the foundation of your house (from a structural stance): on solid ground or sinking sand?

It can also *feel* overwhelming at times to even consider how to budget. There's that word: **budget**.

Let's hop into our learning in this chapter by reflecting on this first key word to see what comes up for you as you continue formulating your vision for financial health and generational wealth!

STOP & JOT

Take a moment to reflect on the following questions. **Reminder:** Each set of *Stop & Jot* questions are designed to help you build out your vision for your optimal financial health.

1. Let's go deeper with the ***C.A.S.H. Financial Health Framework.*** We will zone in on the "C" once again to examine what may need to ***change*** about our mindset. When you hear the word **budget**, what emotion-based words come to mind? **Pro tip*: Don't hold back or judge your immediate thoughts; name and list out all the descriptive thoughts/words that come to mind with the word *budget.*

2. As you examine your list of words/descriptors from question one, what patterns do you notice?

3. You are meeting with a finance adviser after this exercise. How do you want to speak about how you manage your money – your financial health management? Write down all the **actions** that are part of developing your balance sheet and/or budgetary goals.

The truth about a balance sheet is that I personally like the terminology over "budgeting". The word budget can often insight feelings of negativity and restriction. So please know: this chapter is focused on developing a healthy relationship with your balance sheet.

Many of us have been trained to only examine our expenses and liabilities. In other words: *How much do I bring in the door and how much goes out the door?*

The mindset with that would be that many of us are living "wealthy" based upon our balance sheet and may not even realize it it. Call it learned behavior, the psychology of money, or "keeping up with the Joneses", we care about how much we have to our names.

Big Secret: Most people (even working at minimum wage and not self-employed) do earn enough to pay themselves *first* even if it is a small amount! Unfortunately, we are often trained to look at our bank and income statements based on how much we earned.

The Reality: We should all be looking at the end of the **balance sheet**!

To help develop your vision for financial health, I am including our simple *C.A.S.H. Framework Balance Sheet Brainstorm* template. The purpose of this companion tool is to help you begin to engage in monthly reflections on your balance sheet wealth and if you are paying yourself first.

I also won't pretend like this is always easy. This can be a very difficult step in your process. Why? There is a large body of ongoing research that continuously demonstrates that when it comes to humans and money…money is more emotional than LOVE.

Wild!

Author of the bestselling book and Netflix series based upon his book, *I Will Teach You to Be Rich*, Ramit Sethi says it well:

> "Anything important in our lives is emotional. Our relationships are emotional, our work is emotional, and so is our money. One of the misconceptions about money is that it's all math. We believe that there is a mathematically correct answer for questions like, "Should I buy a house or rent one?" or "Should I go to graduate school?" or "Should I take this job?" or "Should I negotiate a higher salary?"
> Sure, doing the math can help you answer these questions, but there's no foolproof formula to making money decisions."
>
> [*View source*: Harvard Business Review. https://hbr.org/2021/08/why-are-we-so-emotional-about-money]

So, when you engage in your reflection process (the pages that follow in this chapter are simply *guides*!), remember these realities and show yourself grace. Beating yourself up or visiting places and spaces in your mind of guilt and shame related to your debts or spending will not help anyone.

It certainly does not help you develop a healthy balance sheet, so be sure that you spend the adequate time in reflection throughout your journey.

It is a life-long dance of learning my friends!

C.A.S.H. FRAMEWORK BALANCE SHEET PLANNER

C.A.S.H. MONTHLY BALANCE SHEET PLANNER

Balance Goal: ______________________ Month: ______________________

INCOME

Date	Description	Amount
Total		

FIXED EXPENSES

Date	Description	Amount
Total		

OTHER EXPENSES

Date	Description	Amount
Total		

INVESTMENTS

Date	Description	Amount
Total		

Recap

	Goal	Actual	Difference
Income			
Expenses			
Investments			
Balance			

Figure 1.4.

INVESTMENTS

Date	Description	Amount
Total		

INCOME

Date	Description	Amount
Total		

FIXED EXPENSES

Date	Description	Amount
Total		

OTHER EXPENSES

Date	Description	Amount
Total		

Recap

	Goal	Actual	Difference
Income			
Expenses			
Investments			
Balance			

As you work through some of the case study, template, and self-reflection exercises I have created for you throughout this book, remember that your process for reflecting on your weekly or monthly balance sheet should suit YOU! My hope is that my tools give you some foundational guidance to help you get started with a financial health vision and ongoing wealth building systems that will work for you and your desired lifestyle.

As a reminder, the chapters do not have to be utilized in any specific order. Of course, we have organized them to help build and scaffold your learning, but there are certainly concepts, exercises, and templates that may resonate with you more than others. Try your best not to get overwhelmed and begin with one step at a time.

BUILDING YOUR BLUEPRINT

In this text we are working towards establishing your vision for optimal financial health. In our *Building a Healthy Balance Sheet* (Chapter 3), we have explored the following terms:

→ **balance sheet**

→ **CASH Financial Health Framework**

→ **budget**

We also spent some time working with reflection questions (*Stop & Jots*) and exercises like our *C.A.S.H. Framework Balance*

Sheet Planner template designed to bring more awareness of your current narratives to the forefront as develop your blueprint.

In the next chapter, we will discuss the four main ways to earn income and some key savings strategies as well as explore our second case study.

SAVING STRATEGIES

CHAPTER 4

As you may have begun exploring what your healthiest balance sheet can look like, I want to direct your attention to the four core methods for earning income:

- Earned income from a job (W2)
- Entrepreneurial endeavors (LLC, S-Corp, etc.)
- Dividends and interest (stocks, bonds, etc.)
- Passive income streams (royalties, real estate, etc.)

Having this base knowledge on types of income and savings strategies will also support your financial health vision as you explore Chapter 6: *Make and Save Money in Your Sleep!*

CONCEPTUAL OVERVIEW: COMPOUNDING

When I share with clients about savings strategies (not always specific to retirement, by the way), I realize that many of us are never explicitly taught about the concept of **compounding interest**.

Let's examine two key definition providers of *compounding* and then dive a bit deeper into application with a case study.

One website I explored out of curiosity was one of the largest American banks, Wells Fargo. Their definition of *compound growth* is:

> "Compounding is a powerful investing concept that involves earning returns on both your original investment and on returns you received previously. For compounding to work, you need to reinvest your returns back into your account."
>
> [*View source*: Wells Fargo. https://www.wellsfargo.com/financial-education/investing/compound-interest-growth/]

The next source is one of the leading online article sources for investing called Investopedia.

> "Compounding typically refers to the increasing value of an asset due to the interest earned on both a principal and accumulated interest. This phenomenon, which is a direct realization of the time value of money (TMV) concept, is also known as compound interest."

[*View source*: Investopedia. https://www.investopedia.com/terms/c/compounding.asp]

TIME IS ON YOUR SIDE

As we explore a few key savings strategies, I cannot stress enough the importance of understanding strategies that have compounding effects.

When most people think about savings strategies they either (1) do not have strategies for saving OR (2) are not taking advantage of the highest-yield model of returns.

Let's **consider certificates of deposit (CD's**). CD's and CD ladders can be powerful strategies that resulting in dividend cycles and compounding interest. However, say that I have $50,000 sitting in a low-interest savings account for 20+ years. I truly don't consider low-interest savings accounts much of a strategy for saving. Buy implementing a CD strategy with that same 50k could result in *thousands* more dollars at a much faster return rate. This is one example of a **compounding interest savings strategy**.

Additionally, the aforementioned type of strategy is considered lower risk and ensures more regular access to funds in a staggered-interval-type disbursement.

With savings strategies, the purpose is to have diversified buckets of money. And this is where our mantra of "pay thyself first" comes into action!

If you determine you can pay yourself 10% of what you earn every time you are paid (*assuming the remaining 90% is already allocated*), you can spread portions of that 10% across things like an emergency fund, retirement accounts, a life-goal or vacation fund, etc. The sooner you start paying yourself first, the more compounding effects you'll experience. When we understand the strategies where we apply our payments to ourselves, we can rest assured that no matter the actual dollar amounts you begin with, you can capitalize on compounding interest models across a variety of strategies to win the long race.

It is like the adage: How do you eat an elephant? *One bite at a time.*

This is why aligning your strategies *with* your vision for financial health will fast-forward your experiences as you are *Walking Your Way to Wealth* (Chapter 8, which is the part of this text where we have *all* the tools to put it all together: developing your financial health vision and aligned roadmap!).

Just remember that it is not a race and if you are competing with anyone, it should only be yourself.

Now, let's explore another one of my favorite savings strategies through another case study: **Roth IRAs**.

THE ROTH IRA CASE STUDY

To engage in some targeted practice and application of utilizing a **financial health vision** as you build your own blueprint, I would like to share this case study with you for your learning, practice, and application.

EDDIE'S ROTH IRA CONUNDRUM

Eddie is 35-years-old and has worked within the same company for the past 6 years. He recently received a promotion which will afford him a pay raise of nearly $20,000 annually. He read my first edition of *Taking Your Financial Pulse* and loved the idea of being able to pay himself first from his weekly checks. He implemented the strategy about one year ago and already took a vacation trip that had been on his bucket list for over a decade!

He remembers that he wanted to implement some type of savings strategy using an IRA.

"Hmmm...I can't quite remember which type has the most favorable compounding interest..." he ponders. "Thank you, Universe, for search engines and AI!"

In his search, he simply requests: *a list of websites that teach about Roth IRAs.*

Here were his findings with overviews and direct article links from his request:

- Fidelity Investments: The Fidelity website provides detailed information on how Roth IRAs work, including rules, benefits, and eligibility criteria.
- CNBC Select: CNBC offers a list of the best Roth IRA accounts for growing money tax-free, focusing on ease of use, customer support, and educational resources.
- The Motley Fool: The Fool's website explains Roth IRA rules, contribution limits, eligibility requirements, and how to get started with a Roth IRA.
- NerdWallet: NerdWallet provides insights into how Roth IRAs work, highlighting differences from traditional IRAs, benefits, fees, account minimums, and promotions.
- Investopedia: Investopedia offers information on what a Roth IRA is, how to open one, the establishment process, investment options, fees, and account requirements.

Citations:

- https://www.investopedia.com/terms/r/rothira.asp
- https://www.nerdwallet.com/article/investing/how-a-roth-ira-works
- https://www.fool.com/retirement/plans/roth-ira/
- https://www.cnbc.com/select/best-roth-ira-accounts/
- https://www.fidelity.com/learning-center/smart-money/how-does-a-roth-ira-work

He takes a coffee break and realizes his head is spinning after about a two-hour daytime detour combing the internet. Then it hits him: *"I need to go back to my foundation: my vision for financial health to consider my approach and where to begin with this specific strategy. Thanks Andy!"*

STOP & JOT

Let's examine Eddie's vision for financial health and what we know about his case study. You will notice with this case study that our questions are more application-based as opposed to introspective. At this point in our journey together, we will start moving from reflecting and learning to more applying and planning. For example, in our first question below I will request that you go explore Eddie's list. I want you to become aware (a.k.a. take a financial pulse!) of how you typically expand your knowledge when it comes to your financial health and find new savings strategies.

1. Using Eddie's list from his research adventures, consider your own understanding of Roth IRAs and utilize the space on the following page to jot down notes, ideas, and/or questions.

____

____

____

____

2. When Eddie found his copy of my book, this is what he had developed as his financial health vision:

Retire by age 50 by prioritizing paying ME first and consistently invest 10% of my paycheck

in compounding interest savings strategies.

Now is when you get to critique Eddie's vision for financial health and steal ideas for your own (hint, hint…Chapter 5!)

In this case study, Eddie's strategy and vision for financial health highlight the common challenges of needing knowledge while still build understanding and application skills with confidence. By returning to his foundation, his vision statement tailored for only him, he can clearly be reminded of what steps make sense for alignment.

In building your blueprint, remember that the best budgeting strategy (*in my opinion!*) is your own personalized and empowered approach to budgeting where you are the hero of your story.

BUILDING YOUR BLUEPRINT

Remember one of our key objectives of this interactive text is to establish your vision for optimal financial health. In our *Saving Strategies* (Chapter 4), we have explored the following terms:

→ **compounding interest**
→ **Roth IRA**
→ **certificate of deposit**

We also spent some time working with reflection questions (*Stop & Jots*) and exercises (like Eddie's "*Roth IRA Case Study*"!) designed to bring more knowledge and practice as your own blueprint begins to come together.

In the next chapter, I will have you begin formulating your vision for financial health by conducting a financial pulse check – personalized inventories which are aligned to the *C.A.S.H. Financial Health Framework*.

FORMULATING YOUR VISION

CHAPTER 5

The biggest assets many will acquire in their lifetime are their house and a 401k. But did you know that only about 30% of employees who are offered 401k options in the workplace actually participate [de Vise, D. (2024) Don't understand your 401(k)? You're not alone, survey shows. *USA Today*].

Another program that often gets overlooked with employers are pension programs where employers often will implement contribution matching. I would consider this a common financial pitfall: thinking your money is more necessary in the immediate than the future by not contributing to employer programs.

We may also categorize milestones in life as "pitfalls" if we are unprepared. Unexpected birth, death, pets, medical events, etc. have the ability to really trip you up in your goals. Being equipped for financial emergencies or drought periods and learning how to build your own financial toolbelt is the answer! **But the biggest pitfall of all? Not learning to pay yourself first.** YOU are the first bill you need to pay every month.

As you work through this chapter, consider how big you are thinking. You have plenty of time and all the options at your fingertips. Let's see what direction you'd like to go first!

APPLYING THE C.A.S.H. FINANCIAL HEALTH FRAMEWORK

As we formulate your vision for financial health, I want you to think back to Eddie's case study (Chapter 4) and his vision for financial health. It is really helpful to think about your statement as a power sentence that you can easily memorize and/or display somewhere meaningful to you. This keeps you focused and "eyes on the prize". This step is so important to your journey! Please take time to review the steps of the *C.A.S.H. Financial Health Framework* prior to using our financial pulse inventory.

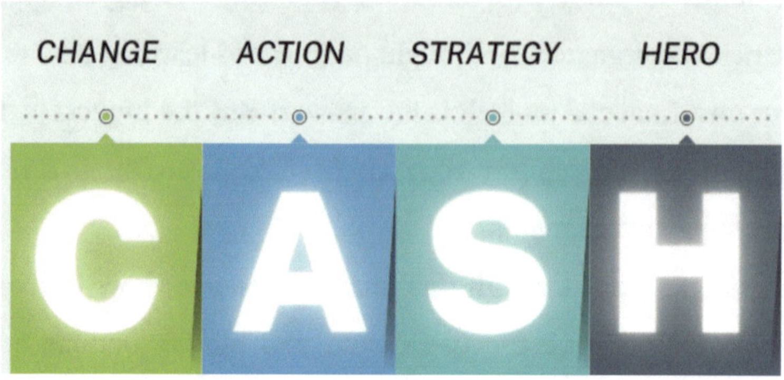

Step 1: CHANGE

CHANGE is about reflecting on your current financial mindset and identifying areas where you feel the need for *change*. This could include attitudes towards spending, saving, investing, or any other aspect of personal finance.

I also encourage you to consider the impact of your current financial mindset on your long-term goals and aspirations. Acknowledge the need for change and commit to embracing a more positive and proactive approach to managing your finances.

Step 2: ACTION

Taking ACTION is all about developing a plan of action to address the areas of your financial mindset that require improvement. This could involve setting specific, achievable goals related to saving, investing, debt reduction, or any other financial priority.

You may consider implementing practical steps to support your plan, such as creating a budget, seeking financial education, or consulting with a professional advisor. Take ownership of your financial journey and commit to consistent action towards positive change.

Step 3: STRATEGY

When you enact the STRATEGY step of the *CASH Financial Health Framework*, you may want to identify specific strategies and tools that align with your financial goals and the areas you wish to improve. This could involve exploring different investment options, debt repayment strategies, or ways to increase your income.

As you will hear me share my honest opinions on budgeting later in this chapter, I want you to tailor any of your strategies to suit your individual circumstances and preferences, ensuring that the strategies you choose are realistic and sustainable for the long term. Most of all: that they are relevant in making you the hero in your own story!

Step 4: HERO

Look at you: embracing the concept of becoming the HERO in your own vision for financial health and generational wealth! Please…REMEMBER that you have the power to shape your financial future through intentional decision-making and a clear focus on your vision for financial health.

Your vision will support you in cultivating a mindset of empowerment and resilience, viewing challenges as opportunities for growth and learning. Commit to being an active participant in your financial journey and strive to inspire positive change within yourself and others.

By using the guidance of the *CASH Financial Health Framework*, you can gain a deeper understanding of your financial mindset and develop a clear roadmap for achieving greater stability, security, and prosperity.

This framework empowers you to take control of your financial well-being and work towards building a legacy of generational wealth through intentional action and strategic planning.

TAKING YOUR FINANCIAL PULSE

In this portion of the chapter, we encourage you to work through each question set as it will guide our work together in Chapter 7 (*Walking Your Way to Wealth)* and you will need this information to utilize the roadmap templates.

For each financial pulse (aligned to the framework), utilize the scale below to tally your response in the column labeled "pulse".

1 = very uncomfortable

2 = uncomfortable

3 = neutral/unsure right now

4 = comfortable

5 = highly comfortable

CHANGE *FINANCIAL PULSE*

C.A.S.H. INDICATOR	PULSE
Managing your current balance sheet.	
Identifying your money worries and wins.	
Long-term savings strategies.	
Implementing personal goals related to money.	

ACTION *FINANCIAL PULSE*

C.A.S.H. INDICATOR	PULSE
Identifying your internalized money mindset.	
Managing investments.	
Implementing a plan for debt management.	
Tracking personal milestones related to money.	

STRATEGY *FINANCIAL PULSE*

C.A.S.H. INDICATOR	PULSE
Seeking out education and advising resources.	
Compounding interest savings strategies.	
Long-term savings strategies.	
Evaluating your balance sheet consistently.	

HERO *FINANCIAL PULSE*

C.A.S.H. INDICATOR	PULSE
Paying myself *first*.	
Developing a vision for financial health.	
Exercising resilience when financial barriers arise.	
Investing in your own education and trying new strategies.	
TOTAL *YOUR CURRENT FINANCIAL PULSE*	

STOP & JOT

Let's take a pause to reflect on the self-reflection process. It may be difficult and/or celebratory to read some of your results. Pay attention and notice how you feel in this moment following the financial pulse check.

In the next chapter, you will utilize your results and reflections in this chapter to help populate your plans and finalize your roadmap for walking your way to wealth and becoming the hero who *always* pays themselves first!

1. Which element of C.A.S.H. (*change, action, strategy, or hero*) do you currently feel ***most*** comfortable with based on your pulse check results?

2. Which element of C.A.S.H. (*change, action, strategy, or hero*) do you currently feel ***least*** comfortable with based on your pulse check results?

3. Without overthinking (*smile)* brainstorm on the following pages the life you would live every day if money were no object. (Think: What you are doing, where are you, who you are with, how you travel, eat, dance, experience life, etc.) Envision your very best DREAM LIFE! **I cannot stress the importance of sitting with this exercise, visualizing, then writing down all the details. Have fun!

BUILDING YOUR BLUEPRINT

In *Formulating Your Vision* (Chapter 5), we have engaged with the four financial pulse surveys aligned to my *C.A.S.H. Financial Health Framework*. I wanted the elements of the framework to intentionally be simple to provide you with reflection and direction prior to using our templates to complete your vision statement and map out your blueprint.

Every chapter has been designed to tap into some broader concepts with you being the main character and focus through our whole journey. How does it feel to be the hero in your own story?

BE YOUR OWN HERO:

WALKING YOUR WAY TO WEALTH

CHAPTER 6

It's all about being the **hero** in your own story. At the hero phase of our framework, you are monitoring and adjusting as necessary to your financial health vision. As a reminder and to bring us full circle, the process can be applied to any situation by engaging the following protocol:

- Identify the element you are seeking to **change**.
    - *Why is it important to you?*
    - *How does it align with your financial health vision?*

- What **action** can you take in the short-term to impact the change you seek?
    - *Is this action high leverage?*
    - *Is the action manageable?*
- How might you consider a long-term **strategy** that will solidify your goal for change being accomplished?

WHAT IS THE "SECRET SAUCE"?

One of the best dispositions I have found to be a "secret sauce" to developing a strong and lasting vision for your financial health and generational wealth is **curiosity**. When we are curious, we explore. We ask questions. And we are willing to research and try new approaches.

Remember how I confessed in Chapter Two (*Budgeting Basics)* that I think keeping a budget can cause stagnation??

All this being said, there are certainly *many* resources and directions you can journey simply by hopping online and utilizing search engines, blogs, and even artificial intelligence systems.

> **One of the best dispositions I have found to be a "secret sauce" to developing a strong and lasting vision for your financial health and generational wealth is *curiosity*.**

MY INTERNET EXPERIMENT…

I decided to do just that. Conducting a broad search on the internet, I simply asked "*What are the top 10 books on finance?*"

Here is one list with consistent titles that seemed to appear across a multitude of cross-checked resources:

- *Think and Grow Rich* by Napoleon Hill
- *MONEY Master the Game* by Tony Robbins
- *The Big Short* by Michael Lewis
- *The Intelligent Investor* by Benjamin Graham
- *The Simple Path to Wealth: Your Road Map to Financial Independence and a Rich, Free Life* by JL Collins
- *The Psychology of Money: Timeless Lessons on Wealth, Greed, and Happiness* by Morgan Housel
- *This Is the Year I Put my Financial Life in Order* by John Schwartz
- *Financially Forward: How to Use Today's Digital Tools to Earn More, Save Better, and Spend Smarter* by Alexa von Tobel
- *The Six Figure Second Income: How to Start and Grow a Successful Online Business Without Quitting Your Day Job* by David Lindahl, Jonathan Rozek
- *A Random Walk Down Wall Street* by Burton G. Malkiel

Citations:

- https://www.inc.com/geoffrey-james/top-10-personal-finance-books-of-all-time.html
- https://money.usnews.com/money/blogs/my-money/articles/best-personal-finance-books
- https://www.investopedia.com/best-finance-books-5093331
- https://www.wecu.com/ranking-the-49-best-money-books-of-all-time/
- https://www.bookey.app/hot-booklist/-top-10-must-read-finance-books-of-all-time

Please know this is not my professional endorsement of any of the aforementioned texts. However, I wanted to model the power of having ***access*** to information. It's where my secret sauce theory on curiosity rings true: use what you have available to start with and begin getting curious about the financial health strategies that appeal most to you.

This will and *should* change over time as you personally and professionally grow and evolve in your life.

Remember in Chapter Three (*Building a Healthy Balance Sheet)* when I shared the research with you that it is proven humans are more emotional about money than LOVE?! This is why getting into a curious disposition about your finances and financial strategies is so important.

You owe it to yourself to be devoted to consistently taking your financial pulse. This is an inside job, friends, and I know even once you start engaging the exercises that have you journaling about your dream life, you will have a foundation designed just for *you* that will help you stay committed, even when curveballs come your way.

TO THE JOURNEY...

If I leave you with nothing else from this text, please remember this charge: **BE YOUR OWN CASH HERO!** Pay yourself *first* and enjoy a bountiful life.

As the great American rock band, Buffalo Springfield, sings: "Nobody's right if everyone is wrong."

Another charge that individuals should take their own initiative with their finances (and now you know a bit of my preferred music tastes! *smile*). Ask questions. You don't know what you don't know!

Also. Don't rely on what markets or finance "gurus" tell you. Sure, it is good to find knowledge and learn from professionals. However, market dynamics, in particular, are so powerful that you will never get a "for sure" or "guaranteed" direction. This is also a common thought process I see people make: thinking a certain strategy is a "sure thing." Simple participation is all that is required when you're the hero in your financial health journey.

Embody being your own financial hero…and don't wait for your bank account to display a specific number before you decide to be your own hero and pay yourself first. Even if it is $1 per week: GET STARTED, heroes!

I will leave you with parting words to ponder and perhaps our paths will cross again:

If you pay yourself first, do you *ever* have to feel as though anything is being *taken* from you?

I encourage you to confidently move forward in your journey and I wish you the very best as you continue to take your financial pulse and maintain a positive trajectory with your vision for long-term financial health and generational wealth.

Simple participation is all that is required when you're the hero in your financial health journey.

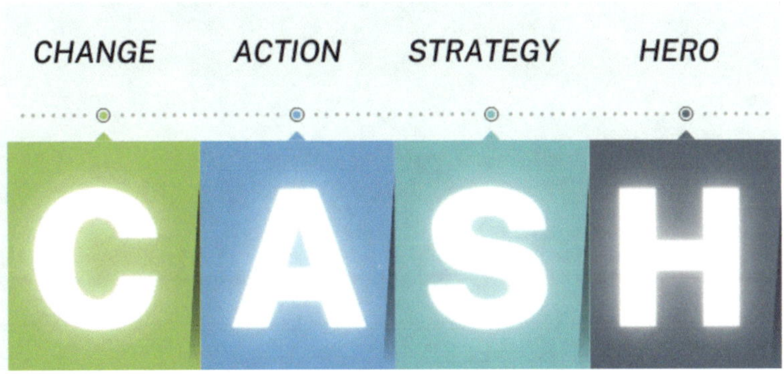

RESOURCES

In this section, I have compiled the *CASH Framework*, all inventories in this text, and the book's two featured case studies.

Whether you want to do a book study with your kids or a trusted confidante, I want you to have easy access to additional copies of all my resources for gathering your thoughts, marking up the texts with your own thoughts, ideas, and vision, while continuously re-visiting your vision for your financial health.

STOP & JOT

Take a moment to reflect on the following questions. As you work through this text, please know that each set of *Stop & Jot* questions are designed to help you build out your vision for your optimal financial health.

1. How often do you spend time focusing on what is *working* in your finances? Why or why not?

2. Identify 1 strategy you currently use consistently for saving. How is it working for you and why does it work for your budgeting style?

3. It is 10 years in the future, and you are living your dream life! What are the things you do every day? Who is with you? How do you earn money?

→ **DREAM BIG!**

STOP & JOT

Take a moment to reflect on the following questions. As you work through this text, please know that each set of *Stop & Jot* questions are designed to help you build out your vision for your optimal financial health.

1. Which do you tend to fixate on *first* when it comes to your bank accounts: how *much* you have or how *little* you have? *Take time to reflect on what this makes you aware of regarding your current mindset.* Does something need to shift?

MONEY WINS/WORRIES **EXAMPLE A**

WIN	WORRY
$500 per week in savings	18k overall credit card debt
$250 per month to 401k account; employer matching	$450 per month car loan payment
3k tax refund	$200 per month student loan
New credit card limit increased with travel rewards points program	Cost of living increases due to increase in property taxes

Figure 1.1.

MONEY WINS/WORRIES

WIN	WORRY

Figure 1.2.

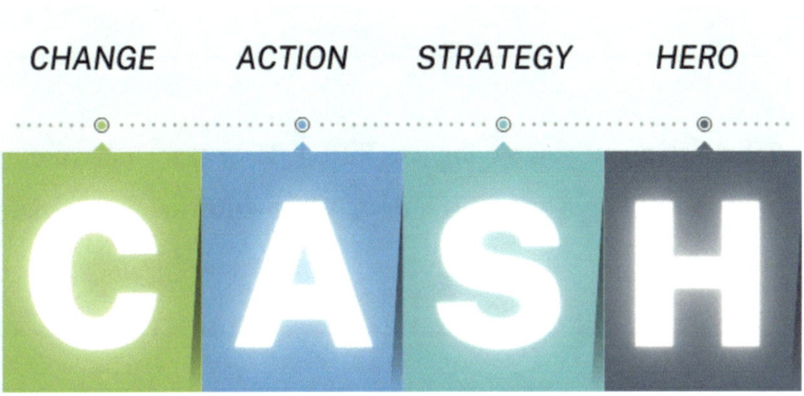

Figure 1.3.

STOP & JOT

Take a moment to reflect on the following questions. As you work through this text, remember that each set of *Stop & Jot* questions are designed to help you build out your vision for your optimal financial health.

1. Let's go deeper with the ***C.A.S.H. Financial Health Framework.*** What are 2 habits you will be implementing to support the **change** you are seeking?

____

____

____

____

____

____

____

2. I am all about **you** paying ***you*** FIRST. How are you becoming the **hero** in your own story each day? What shifts are you noticing in your life?

3. It is 10 years in the future, and you are living your dream life! (*Yes! There is a reason you are seeing this question again!)* What are the things you do every day? Who is with you? How do you earn

money? → **HINT: Get specific about your long-term strategy that has developed generational wealth.**

BUDGETING IS YOUR PERSONAL PREFERENCE [*IMO...*]

Remember what I tell my clients:

> → ***When you pay yourself first,***
> ***it gives you a sense of purpose.***

THE CASH MONEY CASE STUDY

To bring more awareness into your money mindset as you build your blueprint to commit to your financial health vision, I would like to share this case study with you for your analysis and reflection.

SARAH'S CASH MONEY CONUNDRUM

Sarah is a 28-year-old marketing professional who is finding herself in a tight spot when her car unexpectedly broke down. The costly repairs have piled up and she is faced with the urgent need for cash. Due to her current situation, she has been hesitant about her ability to stick to a budget. Even despite having a stable income, Sarah has always struggled with some impulsive spending habits and has never really maintained a consistent budget. I suppose she's like many of us: our money is not a problem until it is a problem.

The idea of restricting her spending and expenses to have enough cash for the car repairs seems overwhelming and she's unsure if she can resist the temptation of unnecessary purchases. Feeling incredibly overwhelmed, Sarah decides to seek advice from a financial counselor to develop a realistic budgeting plan that will allow her to cover the unexpected expenses of her car repairs without compromising her other expenses that she is responsible for.

After consulting with the financial counselor, Sarah now has a better understanding of the importance of budgeting and understanding your balance sheet. With the practical guidance of developing a balance sheet process every month, aligned with her income and spending, she is creating a personalized approach that aligns with her current income needs.

By implementing the recommended strategies, such as tracking her expenses, prioritizing essential costs, and setting aside a portion of her income for savings and investments, Sarah feels more confident in managing her finances. With the support of the budgeting plan and ongoing guidance from the financial counselor, Sarah is successfully navigating the unexpected car situation! Not only is she "taking care of business" – she is developing a healthier outlook with her relationship with money.

STOP & JOT

Take a moment to reflect on the following questions. As you work through this text, please remember that each set of *Stop & Jot* questions are designed to help you build out your vision for your optimal financial health.

1. Let's go deeper with what Sarah is experiencing. Think of a time when you were in a financial crunch or crisis. What tends to be your go-to response?

2. How might you coach yourself through a financial situation that causes you anxiety?

In this case study, Sarah's experience highlights the common challenge of needing cash urgently while lacking confidence in maintaining a budget. Through proactive steps and professional guidance, she was able to overcome her concerns and achieve financial stability, underscoring the value of personalized budgeting strategies.

STOP & JOT

Take a moment to reflect on the following questions. **Reminder:** Each set of *Stop & Jot* questions are designed to help you build out your vision for your optimal financial health.

1. Let's go deeper with the ***C.A.S.H. Financial Health Framework.*** We will zone in on the "C" once again to examine what may need to ***change*** about our mindset. When you hear the word **budget**, what emotion-based words come to mind? **Pro tip*: Don't hold back or judge your immediate thoughts; name and list out all the descriptive thoughts/words that come to mind with the word *budget*.

____

____

____

____

____

____

____

____

____

____

2. As you examine your list of words/descriptors from question one, what patterns do you notice?

3. You are meeting with a finance adviser after this exercise. How do you want to speak about how you manage your money – your financial health management? Write down all the **actions** that are part of developing your balance sheet and/or budgetary goals.

C.A.S.H. FRAMEWORK BALANCE SHEET PLANNER

C.A.S.H. MONTHLY BALANCE SHEET PLANNER

Balance Goal: ____________________ Month: ____________________

INCOME

Date	Description	Amount
Total		

FIXED EXPENSES

Date	Description	Amount
Total		

OTHER EXPENSES

Date	Description	Amount
Total		

INVESTMENTS

Date	Description	Amount
Total		

Recap

	Goal	Actual	Difference
Income			
Expenses			
Investments			
Balance			

Figure 1.4.

INVESTMENTS

Date	Description	Amount
Total		

INCOME

Date	Description	Amount
Total		

FIXED EXPENSES

Date	Description	Amount
Total		

OTHER EXPENSES

Date	Description	Amount
Total		

Recap

	Goal	Actual	Difference
Income			
Expenses			
Investments			
Balance			

THE ROTH IRA CASE STUDY

To engage in some targeted practice and application of utilizing a **financial health vision** as you build your own blueprint, I would like to share this case study with you for your learning, practice, and application.

EDDIE'S ROTH IRA CONUNDRUM

Eddie is 35-years-old and has worked within the same company for the past 6 years. He recently received a promotion which will afford him a pay raise of nearly $20,000 annually. He read my first edition of *Taking Your Financial Pulse* and loved the idea of being able to pay himself first from his weekly checks. He implemented the strategy about one year ago and already took a vacation trip that had been on his bucket list for over a decade!

He remembers that he wanted to implement some type of savings strategy using an IRA.

"Hmmm...I can't quite remember which type has the most favorable compounding interest..." he ponders. "Thank you, Universe, for search engines and AI!"

In his search, he simply requests: *a list of websites that teach about Roth IRAs.*

Here were his findings with overviews and direct article links from his request:

- Fidelity Investments: The Fidelity website provides detailed information on how Roth IRAs work, including rules, benefits, and eligibility criteria.
- CNBC Select: CNBC offers a list of the best Roth IRA accounts for growing money tax-free, focusing on ease of use, customer support, and educational resources.
- The Motley Fool: The Fool's website explains Roth IRA rules, contribution limits, eligibility requirements, and how to get started with a Roth IRA.
- NerdWallet: NerdWallet provides insights into how Roth IRAs work, highlighting differences from traditional IRAs, benefits, fees, account minimums, and promotions.
- Investopedia: Investopedia offers information on what a Roth IRA is, how to open one, the establishment process, investment options, fees, and account requirements.

Citations:

- https://www.investopedia.com/terms/r/rothira.asp
- https://www.nerdwallet.com/article/investing/how-a-roth-ira-works
- https://www.fool.com/retirement/plans/roth-ira/
- https://www.cnbc.com/select/best-roth-ira-accounts/
- https://www.fidelity.com/learning-center/smart-money/how-does-a-roth-ira-work

He takes a coffee break and realizes his head is spinning after about a two-hour daytime detour combing the internet. Then it hits him: *"I need to go back to my foundation: my vision for financial health to consider my approach and where to begin with this specific strategy. Thanks Andy!"*

STOP & JOT

Let's examine Eddie's vision for financial health and what we know about his case study. You will notice with this case study that our questions are more application-based as opposed to introspective. At this point in our journey together, we will start moving from reflecting and learning to more applying and planning. For example, in our first question below I will request that you go explore Eddie's list. I want you to become aware (a.k.a. take a financial pulse!) of how you typically expand your knowledge when it comes to your financial health and find new savings strategies.

1. Using Eddie's list from his research adventures, consider your own understanding of Roth IRAs and utilize the space on the following page to jot down notes, ideas, and/or questions.

____

____

____

____

____

2. When Eddie found his copy of my book, this is what he had developed as his financial health vision:

Retire by age 50 by prioritizing paying ME first and consistently invest 10% of my paycheck in compounding interest savings strategies.

Now is when you get to critique Eddie's vision for financial health and steal ideas for your own (hint, hint…Chapter 5!)

In this case study, Eddie's strategy and vision for financial health highlight the common challenges of needing knowledge while still build understanding and application skills with confidence. By returning to his foundation, his vision statement tailored for only him, he can clearly be reminded of what steps make sense for alignment.

In building your blueprint, remember that the best budgeting strategy (*in my opinion!*) is your own personalized and empowered approach to budgeting where you are the hero of your story.

TAKING YOUR FINANCIAL PULSE

In this portion of the chapter, we encourage you to work through each question set as it will guide our work together in Chapter 7 (*Walking Your Way to Wealth)* and you will need this information to utilize the roadmap templates.

For each financial pulse (aligned to the framework), utilize the scale below to tally your response in the column labeled "pulse".

1 = very uncomfortable

2 = uncomfortable

3 = neutral/unsure right now

4 = comfortable

5 = highly comfortable

CHANGE *FINANCIAL PULSE*

C.A.S.H. INDICATOR	PULSE
Managing your current balance sheet.	
Identifying your money worries and wins.	
Long-term savings strategies.	
Implementing personal goals related to money.	

ACTION *FINANCIAL PULSE*

C.A.S.H. INDICATOR	PULSE
Identifying your internalized money mindset.	
Managing investments.	
Implementing a plan for debt management.	
Tracking personal milestones related to money.	

STRATEGY *FINANCIAL PULSE*

C.A.S.H. INDICATOR	PULSE
Seeking out education and advising resources.	
Compounding interest savings strategies.	
Long-term savings strategies.	
Evaluating your balance sheet consistently.	

HERO *FINANCIAL PULSE*

C.A.S.H. INDICATOR	PULSE
Paying myself *first*.	
Developing a vision for financial health.	
Exercising resilience when financial barriers arise.	
Investing in your own education and trying new strategies.	
TOTAL *YOUR CURRENT FINANCIAL PULSE*	

STOP & JOT

Let's take a pause to reflect on the self-reflection process. It may be difficult and/or celebratory to read some of your results. Pay attention and notice how you feel in this moment following the financial pulse check.

In the next chapter, you will utilize your results and reflections in this chapter to help populate your plans and finalize your roadmap for walking your way to wealth and becoming the hero who *always* pays themselves first!

1. Which element of C.A.S.H. (*change, action, strategy, or hero*) do you currently feel ***most*** comfortable with based on your pulse check results?

2. Which element of C.A.S.H. (*change, action, strategy, or hero*) do you currently feel ***least*** comfortable with based on your pulse check results?

3. Without overthinking (*smile)* brainstorm on the following pages the life you would live every day if money were no object. (Think: What you are doing, where are you, who you are with, how you travel, eat, dance, experience life, etc.) Envision your very best DREAM LIFE! **I cannot stress the importance of sitting with this exercise, visualizing, then writing down all the details. Have fun!

ABOUT THE AUTHOR

Andy Mason is a financial advisor who serves clients desiring to develop a long-term wealth and investment strategy to align with their legacy. Passionate about supporting entrepreneurs in their finance strategies and wealth management, he is a father, husband, and dog lover currently based in the Midwest of the United States.